The warriors who do not fight

The warriors who do not fight

Alison Phipps and Tawona Sitholé

wild goose publications   www.ionabooks.com

Compilation copyright © 2018 Alison Phipps & Tawona Sitholé
Poems by Alison Phipps © 2018 Alison Phipps
Poems by Tawona Sitholé © 2018 Tawona Sitholé

First published 2018 by
Wild Goose Publications,
21 Carlton Court, Glasgow, G5 9JP, UK
the publishing division of the Iona Community.
Scottish Charity No. SC003794.
Limited Company Reg. No. SC096243.

ISBN 978-1-84952-600-5

cover photo and interior photos © Gameli Tordzro

Arts & Humanities Research Council
www.ahrc.ukri.org

All rights reserved. Apart from the circumstances described below relating to non-commercial use, no part of this publication may be reproduced in any form or by any means, including photocopying or any information storage or retrieval system, without written permission from the publisher.

Non-commercial use: The material in this book may be used non-commercially for worship and group work without written permission from the publisher. If photocopies of small sections are made, please make full acknowledgement of the source, and report usage to the CLA or other copyright organisation.

Alison Phipps & Tawona Sitholé have asserted their rights in accordance with the Copyright, Designs and Patents Act, 1988, to be identified as the authors of this work.

Overseas distribution
Australia: Willow Connection Pty Ltd, Unit 4A, 3-9 Kenneth Road, Manly Vale, NSW 2093
New Zealand: Pleroma, Higginson Street, Otane 4170, Central Hawkes Bay
Canada: Novalis/Bayard Publishing & Distribution, 10 Lower Spadina Ave., Suite 400, Toronto, Ontario M5V 2Z2

Printed by Bell & Bain, Thornliebank, Glasgow

Contents

Introduction	9
daydreaming in darkness	12
Finding a way for our dreams	14
the challenge	16
Black skin. White masks	17
border crossing in Togo (insert place of choice)	18
It wasn't elephant grass, was it?	20
imMigration	22
The academic border guard	25
victor's storybook	28
If you say my name	30
it so happened	32
A war story	34
the boy at the ferry	36
A pebble. Lesbos	37
disturbing dreams	40
Poem for the careful days	41
customs and exile	44
My name is Alison, … and I am a recovering racist	46

as arrows take to flight	49
A day to rest from war	51
of silence	53
White gifts of the dark night	54
cold insignia	55
Winter solstice approaches	56
cape coast caper	57
Cape ghost	67
after the storm	70
Translating the rain	71
happening	73
The next wound	74
from within	75
From the storm to the sea	77
documentarity	78
New York Public Library	79
dance to survive	82
Desert museum	84
community	86
Visiting Mercy	87
wish i'd known better	89
Healtime	90

inWARdly	93
Courage is made in times like this	94
look right look left	95
We will not let you pass	96
meet me at the corner	98
An upper room	99
my-views-news reporter	101
After this restless house	103
new dogs old tricks	107
The one you feed	109
not meant for words	111
The end of reason	112
t a B l e t s	113
I went to the trees	114
voice versa	115
This music	116
border	119
Daffodils	120
broken world, broken word	122
The spring	124
Acknowledgements	126

Introduction

In September 2015 the world woke up to the fact that, for well over a decade, people seeking refuge from war and persecution were drowning by their thousands in the Mediterranean.

From sub-Saharan Africa and conflicts across the Middle East bodies moved, died or survived.

This is the epic story of exile – one of biblical proportions, one told by the Ancients and the Ancestors.

This book is an intimately woven conversation – which began in Ghana where we were working for UNESCO and the Arts & Humanities Research Council (AHRC) – of two friends bearing witness to war and the suffering of their peoples.

One black; one white. One of the north; one of the south.

This is a cycle of grief and life. We are both, in our own traditions, people of prayer; venerators of the cycle of the seasons and the wisdom of books, prophets and elders. In an echoing call and response we offer words for these times of war; ways of wondering what it means to resist; to suffer with; to bear witness; to seek companionship; to govern the tongue; to defy; to hold counsel; to be part of the agony of a family made in love, and parting, separated by land, sea and paperwork.

In language redolent of nature and strong words of old, we beat out rhythms from the suffering of hearts longing for wartime to end, the dreams of peace to begin and for those we love to live well, to come close, and break bread.

Written from airports while waiting for loved ones to arrive, in the depths of the rainforests of Ghana and Aotearoa New Zealand, in Zimbabwe and the stunted remains of the Caledonian and Atlantic rainforests, from gardens and offices, gun emplacements and slave forts, waiting rooms and checkpoints, at walls and during the upheaval of protests and election campaigns, the words reach into this moment of time: this wartime.

About the cover and illustrations

The cover and illustrations in this book are photographs of a *kente*, a traditional, handwoven cloth from Ghana. The abstract symbols and designs of a *kente* have strong meanings. This image is *niata*, meaning double-edged sword. The sword can be sheathed to bring peace; and drawn to bring war. For warriors who do not fight *niata* is a symbol of the commitment to non-violence, readiness for struggles for justice, and the disciplines of love, which are in the heartbeat of the warriors who do not fight.

The *kente* was made by an unknown *kente* weaver in Kumasi Bonwire, Ghana, and was provided by Naa Densua Tordzro, Fashion Designer and Freelance Artist. The photographs were taken by Gameli Tordzro.

Alison Phipps and Tawona Sitholé

Like the kentenwenenwom *of* kente *weavers and the waulking songs of Gaelic women, these poems work as a call and response, or echo.*

We have differentiated authorship by font. The first poem in the collection is by Tawona, the responding poem by Alison, and so on.

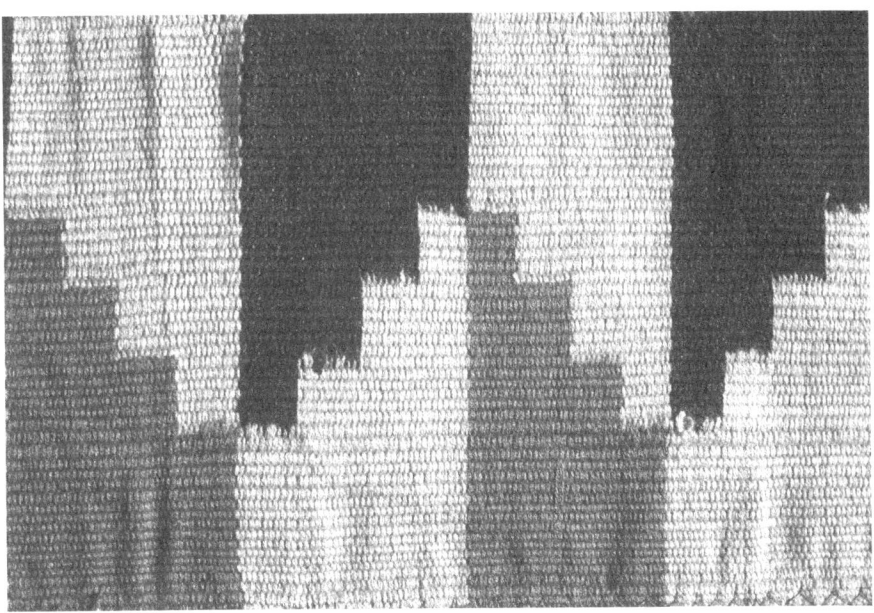

daydreaming in darkness

who shouted *daybreak*
in the middle of the night
that was just me
daydreaming in darkness
but when i'm awake
i see shadows of silhouettes
training for occupation
it was not real work
and it was not really working
yet words so convincing
looks so convincing
if seeing is believing
then i disagree with my eyes

who shouted *liberty*
in the middle of oppression
that was just me
again
daydreaming in darkness
but when i'm awake
i see mixed messages
from the mixed-up messenger
and speeches lengthening
and lessons lessening
yet words so convincing
looks so convincing
if seeing is believing
then i disagree with my eyes

who shouted *unity*
in the middle of separation
that was just me
once again
daydreaming in darkness
but when i'm awake
i see division and inequality
the mathematics of reality
even in another time
averages would be mean
yet words so convincing
looks so convincing
if seeing is believing
then i disagree with my eyes

who called for *celebration*
in the middle of misery
that was just me
yet again
daydreaming in darkness
but when i'm awake
i see nothing
nothing but things hot off the press
that make the blood run cold
i see ignorance sitting pretty
and wisdom sitting lonely
yet words so convincing
looks so convincing
if seeing is believing
then i disagree with my eyes

Finding a way for our dreams

For Kofi

Finding our way
into the memories
of a place where words
were born, and born
bare against the white
skin of the page.

Finding our way forwards
towards words strong enough
for this growing child
the hungry one at my breast,
drinking me wet then dry.

Finding our way
when the way is lost,
when wartime means
that the way
planned
and marked on the map
is no longer a way.

When death is the way;
and there is no path;
and the footsteps
of the ancestors tell
only of the way they came
to bring us to this point.

When the way is
not the way.
And the path
is just a wandering
across the moorland
to the salt marsh
we will water
with our tears.

Today, just enough,
that's all. A diet
of words that nourish
and nurture the only
art that matters,

the art of living
and loving.

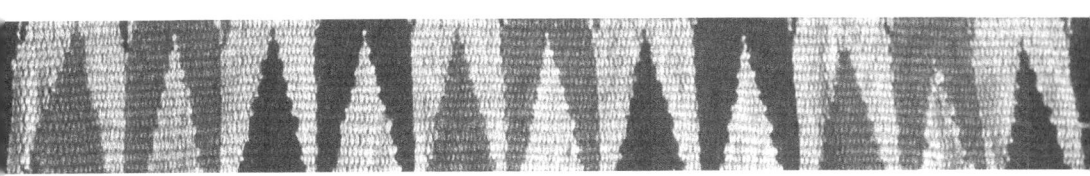

the challenge

if what culture is
is different ways of seeing things
and what language is
is different ways of saying things
then the challenge is
to gather these
different ways to fight challenges

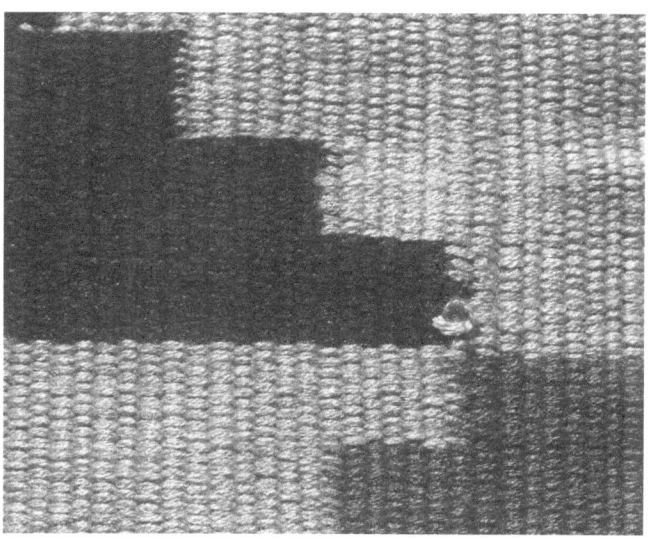

Black skin. White masks

Woke early to glory.

For a moment across
the carpet of islands and
kingfisher sea
no trace of war.

Family sleeping.
Dawn light.

So I turn to my book
and begin reading.

Black skin.
White masks.

Wartime returns
granting that
deeper peace
of pain.

Turning my skin
into yours.

Into ours.

border crossing in Togo (insert place of choice)

there is no one to check you in
or check you out
no one to weigh your baggage
or touch you up
no body in booth
hands above head
feet behind line
there is no unheard of herd of people
no holding pens
no paper cuts
no board no number
no pass no gate
there is no priority clearance
no catwalk for the privileged
no eeh you and non eeh you
no dignity-stripping interview
no very very verification
of identity
ko iwe
ndiwe ani
nhai iwe
wobvepi
ko nhai iwe
woendepi
no receptors no detectors
no specialised interceptors
no thermal scanners

scanning for super diseases
in fact there's only us
only us and the trees
and elephant grass
for now
in a manner of speaking
in a matter of seconds
we're across the frontier
border crossing in Togo

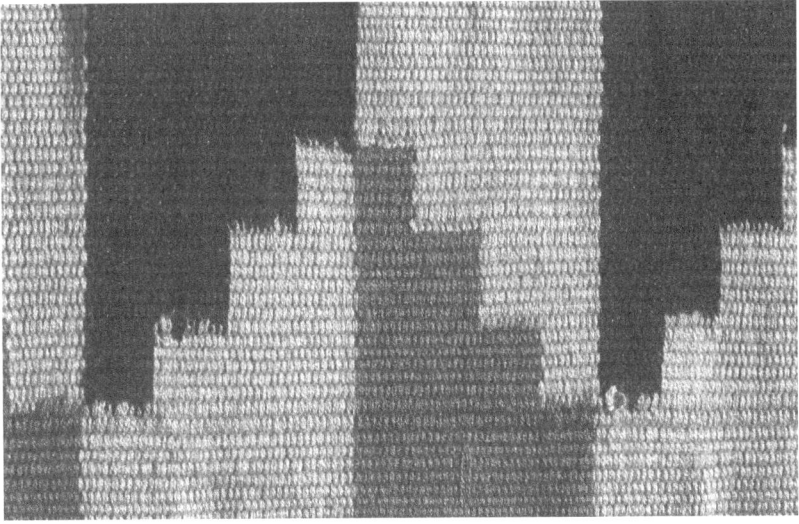

It wasn't elephant grass, was it?

It wasn't elephant grass, was it?
Surely it was flax?
And the ground was stony
and my feet bare
   close to the broken road.

I was just
walking
across a road
   into a field
and there were
friends
   with me
and our
skin was on fire
because the day
was pregnant with
gifts coming
      close to their time.

   You knew we stood
   on hallowed ground.
      As did I.

The natural ditch between
a road and a field
   is a place where
      magic and mischief
         have always been made.

There were admonishments,
but they were laughing
not fearful.

There were remonstrations
but they only served
to strengthen the resolve
and the sense of safety.

I saw no elephants in the grass
    no snakes or angels either.

But the flax was growing
    the twine which would
        weave enchantments,
opening this improbable ground
    beneath our bare feet
to be another
    unstoppable conduit
        for the stories between us
    about to be born.

imMigration

i'm not the stillness
not the quiet
i'm the restless
i'm the sound
i'm the quickening
of heartbeat
the deepening
of breath
i'm the slowing
of motion
i'm the distance
endurance
i'm a thousand hooves
thundering an open plain
i'm a thousand wingbeats
buffeting a yawning sky
i'm an ant
crawling up a giant tree
i'm the flower to flower
stripes of a bee
i'm a worm digging
fish swimming
upstream
i'm the current
i'm times and places
songs and stories

i'm a young pip
an old ship
i'm the source of spices
the illusion of crisis
i'm legs outstretched
flying business class
i'm limbs tucked in
riding as underclass
i'm trains and platforms
waves and sandstorms
i'm the trickle of a stream
through a desert floor
i'm the burst of a flood
through a land of war
i'm the free flow
of goods and cash
i'm the see-saw
of moods perhaps
i'm wine bars
i'm jail bars
i'm official
unofficial
i'm security
insecurity
i'm on the mind
the agenda
i'm on the menu
i'm news

i'm a nuisance
i'm an instinct
i'm water crossing skin
words leaving tongues
i'm breath leaving lungs
breath leaving lungs

The academic border guard

And they will say of me
that despite it all, I was a border guard.
That I assigned my name to the papers
which monitored and revealed the whereabouts
of students from other lands, whose learning
was in my care.

And they will have evidence,
when they look again, once again,
at the only question we can ever have
of history,
'How did this happen?
How can human beings
do this?'

They will say it of me and of my friends
and also of those who comply easily
and don't question, as I do, as I do daily.

They will say it also of those
who made the new rules gleefully
rejoicing in expulsions.

Maybe they will look at
my practices of resistance,
but I doubt it,
the weighing of evidence is rarely
that subtle in such matters
of life and death, as implicate me now.

Maybe they will read the minutes
of the Graduate Studies Committee
of 2007 where we said 'No.'
Maybe they will
examine my chaotic filing system,
my resistance to demands, the way
I spoke to those I am to sign off.
Maybe my accuracy will be found wanting.
But I doubt it. That is probably
not my way, even if I might wish it
to be so.

If justice comes quickly, hopefully
they will say it to my face.
It will help with the healings,
the clearing away of the detritus of the past.

If there is forgiveness in that future,
the one for which I work and pray,
then perhaps they
will say it kindly, and see that,
on balance, I was 'only doing my job'.

These, of course, are the words which
haunt me most.

But if truth be told, my truth be told,
every time I sign my name, I know my
guilt, and shame and believe, that

when the day comes,
and the question is asked,
and the just verdict falls,
for every form filled out
and signed

you should spit in my face.

And if I am dead, then
desecrate my grave
with my guilt.

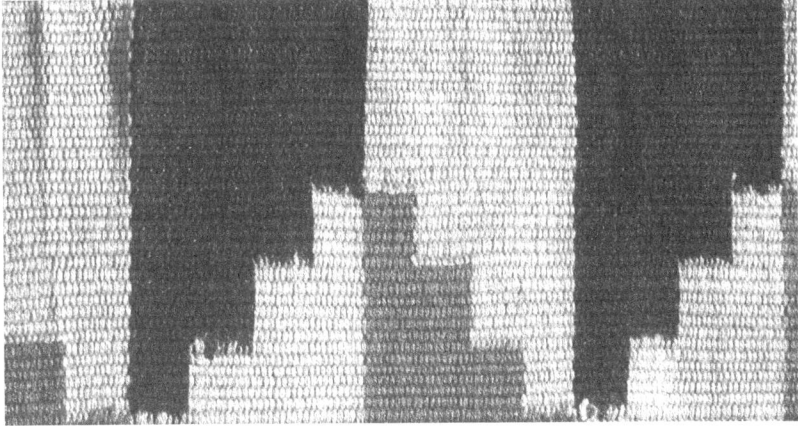

victor's storybook

the big bad wolves are gone
but we're still in a danger zone
nasty and frightful crooks
lie concluded in victor's storybook
but we're still not off the hook
heard that slavery was abolished
but the master's shoe
just can't do without a shine and polish
that is maintenance
new editions with new additions
appear and reappear
with the latest and greatest
mighty search parties sent in the dark
to decorate the sky with furious sparks
but not much illumination
not many enlightened
but most very well red
a mother's cry
a father's silent prayer
and still the stubborn wounds
can't help but fester
some dying from needs
others for no need
and still the common tunes
can't help but pester
the marks of dog ears

facilitate a smooth return
to the most revisited pages
the united nations that are at war
over the common wealth
and through this wilderness
many drift
sometimes lost
and sometimes unaware
that they are lost

If you say my name

Gifts are in the feet.

They bring your voice to my ear.

Tears are in the hair,
your hand helps them
rise through my breath.

War wounds abound
and strength is here
abundantly.

But if you say my name
the world of death
where I stand on a shoreline
with the drowned
where I kneel in the smoking
rubble with the bombed.

If you say my name
where I shake,
barefoot,
on the shards of glass
scattered across the bedroom,

where I listen in to the words
which wound with accusation,
disappointment,
blame and anxiety.

If you say my name
when the letter comes,
and the key turns and the decision falls
and she is taken away.

If you say my name
as you said her name
in the garden,
after the battle,
after death was done
and after war wounds
were wrapped in balm and shroud.

If you say my name.

Gifts are in the feet.

If you say my name.

Tears are in the hair.

War wounds abundantly.

If you say my name.

Say my name.

it so happened

the farmer leads out his cow
and gets his plough
but the earth does not yield
how can this be
he asks
this very land
same land
has fed all
people, animals that live here
trees that grow here
rivers that flow through here
mountains that sit here
from then till now

the singer takes out his instrument
clears his throat
but the song does not come
how can this be
he asks
this musical voice
same voice
has been with many souls
joy that abounds here
pain that is felt here
sentiments that live here
from then till now

the lovers share a bond
but the seed does not come
how
they each ask
can this be
so many generations
have seen regeneration
children that play here
adults that care here
elders that unite here
from then till now

the people prepare for the futuristic
but it never arrives
when
they wonder
will time favour their quests
with favourable answers
changes emerge horizontal
yet knowledge remains
dissolved in the daylight
raindrops fall on all
yet wisdom remains
dissolved in the moonlight
the earth provides
free will decides
life remains a secret
to a choice that chose secrecy

A war story

It's a war story.

A woman
takes an apple
from a tree
tastes
and shares.

It is what women
always do.

It is how
the children
are fed.

But sharing
destroys greed,
destroys the myth
of scarcity,
drives out fear,
distributes power.

So the story
became the war.

And shame
was hers.
And pain
was hers.

And for centuries
knowledge
could not
be hers.

And snakes
were to feast
unbidden
on her body.

And she would
always be to
blame.

Apples –
the root
and branch
of peace
a weapon in
an unjust war.

Come taste,
share, see.

The apple.
The sharing.
Her tender,
knowing gesture,
it starts
His war.

the boy at the ferry

his voice is cool and clear
like the water he is selling
his words are deep and dear
like this river we are crossing
his presence has a sense
intense as the heat
eyes red and magnetic
like the dust on his feet
his words flow freely
jagged though they are
telling a tough story
but not with any fear
words flow freely
like the waters of the Volta
then he reaches in
and pours another smile
he doesn't want a handout
not even a hand
he doesn't push for a sale
not even a bargain
there is no want
no need
just what is understood
it's nearly time
time to go
there is a song between us

A pebble. Lesbos

For Pinar

A pebble.

A stone with
a story.

Here
were hands
first clutching
at waves
clutching
at air.

Then
clutching
at body
at bone
at skin.

On this stone she
knelt, holding
a child, not
dead nor
alive.

On this beach
between worlds

of the living
worlds
of the dead
she held
out her hands.

The body
grey
as the pebble
grey as the
life
draining
back from
the tideline
back into
the lungs
of the sea
grey as
the sky
when weeping.

She knelt.

Her hands
warm.

Her shaking
body and fear
enough to
bring a
jolt of life.

Air rush.

The sound
of crying.

The sound
of life,
of earth,
leaving water,
meeting sky.

The stone
touches my hand.

Giftgrey.

The sky weeps
with my eyes.

The fear I hold
returns to
the sea.

Three women stand
on the shoreline.

Stones.

    Stories.

        History.

disturbing dreams

disturbing dreams
of the future past
give me what i don't need
but look away now
or else witness
disturbing dreams
busy
disturbing dreams
handshakes
handbrakes
hands wave
sands pave
the mind is revealed
only by admission
the heart is revealed
only by permission
images pain themselves
in the blood
images paint themselves
in the dark
difficult as the climb
at a height
humanity echoes
humanity recurs
in the fight of the heart
do as wish
but
leave as is

Poem for the careful days

For Ellie

The breath left her that night.
The visitors tearing at her mind
both angels and demons
locked in mortal combat.
Hot and cold.

Without breath she took to water.
The silky cloak slipping over tired skin.
The visitors did not go quietly.
Each stroke forward made in silence
invaded by a cacophony
of anger and regret.

A day waiting, watching,
filing the thoughts,
removing each visiting demon
from its ancient lock on love.
This one guilt, disappointment,
that one desire, jealousy, self-pity,
this one fear,
that one a carving in ice.

Steadying the greed into grief,
into quiet,
is no small task.
The myth-makers told stories

of those called into the labyrinths
of this quest.

The Ancients called it
binding the strong man.
An instruction
from the greatest teacher of all,

to men.

'Unless he first binds the strong man'
the warning words
to all serious seekers
of freedom
and forgiveness.

But for a woman of poverty
how is this unless-task
to be accomplished?
Another instruction reported for Him
and not Her.

Hidden in the stories,
behind the instructions
are the ways women have taken.

Pondering these things in their hearts,
singing their poverty and humility,
delighting in an invitation,
finding freedom in obedience,
and transgression, and touch.

Resistant, surprising, sensuous,
fiercely silent and spoken.
Their eyes soft with sorrow
and flashing with the ways of life.

A jar of scented oil.
Hair.
Tears on skin.
The countering actions of love.
She too binds the strong man.

Night falls again.
Sleep throws up its walls
and dreams are distant echoes
in the healing mind.

Unmasked and named
for what they are –
angels, fallen,
demons of zeal,
rushing into the cliffs
of the dangerous mind.

Bound for now.

Peace.

Preparing their new drums
for war.

customs and exile

made in
could be anywhere
anywhere in the world
FRAGILE: HANDLE WITH CARE
but what do these symbols mean
THIS SIDE UP
but what do these symbols mean
but some packages come unlabelled
just a bit scuffed
a bit bashed
it now then is upon them
the officers and officials
their job
their duty
their choice
to place a suitable label
on the undefined cargo
based on experience
and what is understood
accepted
expected
they survey the package
they look at the options
there are a lot of stickers
to choose from
a lot of sticky stickers

so strong
once stuck
becomes part of the package
KEEP OUT OF THE REACH OF CITIZENS
but what do these symbols mean
DO NOT EXCEED RECOMMENDED DOSE
but what do these symbols mean
MIGRANT
IMMIGRANT
FOREIGN
REFUGEE
NON-WHITE
ASYLUM SEEKER
ILLEGAL

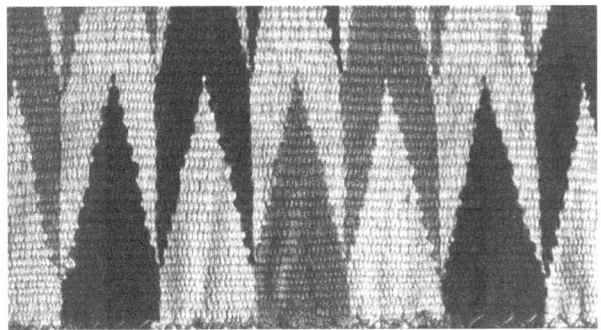

My name is Alison,
... and I am a recovering racist

But I was born with this addiction
because my ancestors were white
and the country
I am from grew fat
in every imperial fight.

Money, privilege and power
come down the barrel of a gun.
That wasn't just in history
it's still how this is done.

The work which calls me loudly
towards your skins and eyes and tears
is the work which is intention
to assuage those birthright fears.

So do not idolise my actions
do not praise my words as bold
do not look at the donations
or the papers that I hold.

The thoughts I have of charity
are just part of this addiction
inherited from a line
that is a long and bleached-out fiction.

I do not have to worry when my skin
is in a room,
or on a train,
or in a car,
or in the immigration tomb.

I will be given space and money
and more time,
because I'm white,

because my ancestors were slave owners,
or slave drivers
and right.

While you, my friends, my kindred
will be skinned another way,
flayed into diminishments
through ever greater punishments
and all those cruel admonishments.

The only proper meaning
of the white man's burden
is that for all my days commitment
will be to a healing labour.

On my deathbed, in my dying
I will be a racist too.
But it's shouldering the burden
that will lead to something new

something giving and forgiving
of the shame upon my skin
something real and raw and honest
that can live with history's sin

not denial of what sticks to
every tone, or shade or pore
but the making of relationships
that brim with something more.

At times our conversation
will make our skins dissolve
and around us through the laughter
a new world may revolve
when the tears are all that join us
when the skin gives way to bone

and through the pain we'll love again
and call this earth our home.

as arrows take to flight

as arrows take to flight
and shadows wake to fight
witnesses may delight
in the promising sight
in the will of untreated ills
borrowing wings from the wind
to shrug off the tug of gravity
in this language of fear power
hissing fizzing whizzing
and whatever else may be
there is turbulence
the mutterings have started
the rustling of leaves
scattering of the startled
the business of unrest
the wounded-to-be
on their way to being scarred
the survivors-to-be
on their way to being scared
and whatever else may be
there is turbulence
ripened fruits soured by time
easily fall off trees
as do
dry leaves devoured by the sun
somewhere up ahead
the backward momentum caused

when two motions collide
hidden symbols
are open wounds
piercing
like a sharp tongue
to cut a long story short
there is impact

A day to rest from war

A day to rest from war.
A walk from the battlefield
to a lonely dale
where the arrows hover
on the horizon
like the mist
present but
not piercing the skin.

A day to tend the weariness
of wartime.
To feel the wounds one
after another.
A day to talk of war
and warriors
as the eagle soars.

Absence of war makes
the presence of
wounds
press into bone,
press into blood.

Absence of war
brings the carrion crows.
Murmurations of migrating birds,
like unleashed arrows,
criss-cross the skies.

The warriors who do not fight

A day to rest.

Feel the wounds.

Watch the arrows in their
expectant formations
overhead.

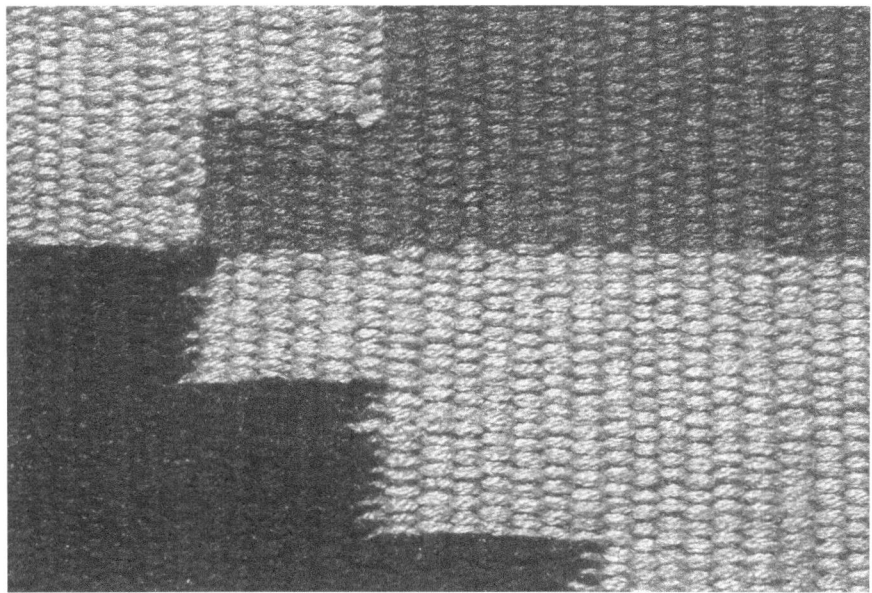

of silence

speaking of silence is breaking it
better to observe
yet another movement
but some things remain still
and since the past cannot be altered
only disputed
let's play
and since the other senses are alive
especially hope
let's practise
freedom of speech
is a basic human risk
silence is a thin blanket
that covers my dreams
silence is a thick blanket
that protects my dreams
who i am
where i am from
how i came
to be here
my closed eyes squeeze the truth
if this lid be lifted
they will hear my secret songs

White gifts of the dark night

The body offers itself to its changes,
ceases its wrestling,
and the mind hides,
for a moment,
from the danger it needs to impose.

The rain clouds retreat.
Stars pierce the sky again.
Night begins its cold work
hardening the water, the ground.

In the dreams are memories.

In the waking hours,
as weak light lengthens
the garden shows
the lacework of the air,
the mist, the night.

Questions wake to fractal answers.
Crystals cling to bronze and gold.

The moon shyly softens the fearful heart.
Cold smiles because she now knows
that such are the white gifts
of dreamtime and the dark night.

Such is the secret
when the war grows old.

cold insignia

cold insignia
so cold
seeing it
can make the eyes shiver
so cold
feeling it
can make the soul quiver
where it strikes
way it lingers
see you in winter

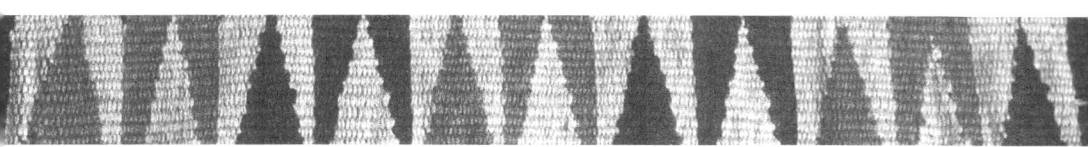

Winter solstice approaches

There are few days left
in this inexorable plunge into darkness.
The trees appal with cold skin
their coats rotting in the rain.
The people cover their smiles, their eyes.

The wren hides in the hedge, shy yet seen.

I cling still to the lingering light,
walking the labyrinth from edge to edge.
The maze a felt metaphor
for the way of desperation.
The feet take the words
and step by step the light
grows weaker still.

Across cold northern continents
the light follows the wren.

The blackbird has lost her song.

Deep darkness will soon be upon us.
Now it is time to release our need for light.

In these the darkening days,
these days of dying,
these days of killing,
these days of drowning,
these the days of declaring
another war.

cape coast caper

if there is one thing
about this place
it's the noise
the many many volumes
of history
the rusty rusty ringing
of decibels
the ruthless lashes
of the waves
the fiery rage
of the sea
the high-pitched voices
of the traders
trying
to shout above each other
trying
to shout above the noise
it's more than you can stand

in the discord
the wind is whistling

you must leave it here
your name
you must leave it here
otherwise
they won't let you past

and so you do
and as you enter

in the discord
the wind is whistling

gold coast cape coast
put on your mask
put on your mask
for the mask-eraid
gold coast cape coast
put on your cape
put on your cape
for the escapade
the mass parade
the mass parade
they all line up for
the mass parade

and as they fade
what appears to be your guide appears
and starts walking
instinctively you follow the momentum
but this only leads to a stall
with percussive triangles
with shirts and blouses
with hearts on sleeves
fancy tightrope
to skip a generation

soothing lotions
and
calming creams
to rub on wounds
and paste on scars
it's more than you can take

the guide is speaking
but is drowning
in the discord
instead
what you can hear
is a spirited voice
not loud
but crisp
against the noise

this is not why i came
this is not what i came
to be
known as
known for

a shadow steals by
can't tell whether
a vendor
defender
or
pretender

the one thing about this place
is the appearance
facing the sea
the darkened house
with whitewashed walls
with rooms rooms
passages and guns
pointing in all directions
at invisible enemies
and beneath
the courtyard
tunnels tunnels
cavities and cells
with no
no window
you could swear
this house is darkening
you could swear
these walls are whitening
it's more than you can stand

in the discord
the wind keeps whistling

the mask-eraid
the escapade
they all line up for
the mass parade

and as they fade
you wonder whether
the other visitors
can see them too
the shadows
and the more you look
the less you see
the less there seems to be

the guide is walking
instinctively you follow the momentum
but this only leads to another stall
with hides hidden
in exquisite bracelets
in a variety of complexions
shades and tones
some for wrists
some for ankles
some for minds
it's more than you can take

the guide is speaking
but is drowning
in the discord
instead
what you can hear
is a spirited voice
not loud

but clear
above the noise

borrowed time
has side effects
and too many to count
like visits of the tide

another shadow steals by
can't tell whether
a dweller
seller
or
sell-out

the guide is walking
instinctively you follow the momentum
but this only leads to another stall
with refreshments
special brew
a blend
of floods
of held-back tears
of cocktails
of emotions
one sip
sharp taste
two sips
bitter taste
it's more than you can take

the guide is speaking
but is drowning
in the discord
instead
what you can hear
is a spirited voice
not loud
but clean
across the noise

when will this end
in fact
when will this begin
i don't want to leave
but
take me to another place

one thing about this place
is the atmosphere
only thing that comes close
is the utmost fear
just like a restless survivor
the air is never still
and
between areas of pressure
winds keep blowing
nothing more chilling
than a trade wind
that keeps whistling
after the home is blown

and this one lingers
on the opaque walls
between
long unbroken silences
between
quiet solemn reflections
some of what is
blown in
some of who are
blown away
in the
unending argument
between land and sea

land is solid
water is fluid
sun is smiling
wind is whistling
and
heart is beating

seems like any other
ordinary day
but this is not any other
ordinary place
on any day
at any time
by any law
in any tongue

what happened
happens
here
lies beyond
this final
point of
the tour
the door
of no return

in the discord
you seem to hear
what seems to lie
beyond
seems like
the wind is whistling
not sure if
the voices are
sounds of harm
or
harmony

gold coast cape coast
put on your mask
put on your mask
for the mask-eraid
gold coast cape coast
put on your cape
put on your cape

for the escapade
the mass parade
the mass parade
they all line up for
the mass parade

Cape ghost

For Obed

Which one haunts you?
Is it an ancestor
or the captive screaming of today?

Is there whiteness in your skin,
is there blame?

Which voices do you hear
from the death mask's whisper?
Was the blood you share
a trader?
Was the blood you share
a slave?

Which shadows do you see
in the gate of no return
behind the door of no return?

Are you the one he saw,
chose,
bathed and
screaming through
a trapdoor
screaming
from the trapped door
bore his now creaming child?

Are you the one whose eye
was choosing, following
skin and limb and
glowering
holding hand to hip
to mouth
in the tearingtaking
that is war?

Are you the trader who
measured angles
clasped shackles
taking the way of wrangles?

Are you the girl child,
the boy child
your mother plucked
for the fields of the south,
and you for lands to the north
her memory a brand
like the one
on your skin?

Are you the preacher
of Zion
blessing abomination
before you proudly trade
in the name of a god?

Are you the guide, traveller
in time, telling the flattened
endlessly repeating
tales of terror,

closing the door
of no return
on those
who pay to know?

Cape Coast

the sea is coming to
greet you,

which ghost
are you?

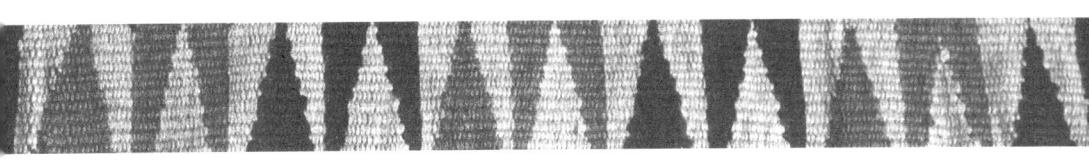

after the storm

after the storm
all seems calm
so much is torn
safe from harm

Translating the rain

For Rosco

It's a war dance.
The drummers have taken
to the trees.
Every beat signals a move
and a message.

On the roof
the rain urges us to stay
in this shelter house
while the storm sends
time
out of time.

The thunder sends signals
for translating the rain.

We translate the rain.
Whirl, dip
stamp, twist
wild,
    wild,
        wild.

A battle storm
between a border
and a breath

the wildness of dreamtime
echoing wartime
preparing the body, the soul
for the harder beating of the
bounds that make
for the wideness
of peace.

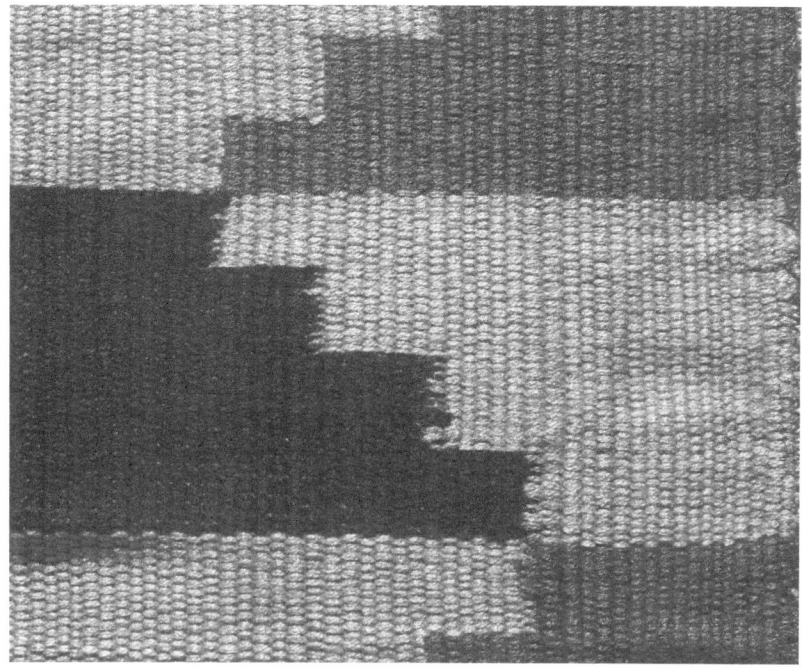

happening

the future is uncertain
but it is certain
that it is coming
reality is unclear
but it is clear
that it is happening
words can't stop it
yet words can't stop
talking to despise
only clothing a prisoner
living in disguise
meantime
drum with worn skin
beating strong again
to celebrate life
in the company of friends
in the arms of family

The next wound

In wartime
each poem arrives
by grazing the heart
like a well-aimed arrow
deflected by chance.

In wartime
each poem takes you through
to a sanctuary
surrounded
by drumming
and cries.

In wartime
there are wounds
sliced open by arrows,
made in words,
aching for the sound
of the whip and
air-rush
the arrival
of the next
wound.

from within

from within
skin
for without
kin
just withering
shivering
reeds in current
akin
to dithering
mother tongue
wean me
only if you cease
warn me
only if you please
wake me
only when you dream
glorious symbols
patterns
in the folds
between two cloths
one
the colour of water
one
the other
the colour of forests
one
another

entwined
in time
of war
a warrior's weapon
a warrior's beacon
is another warrior

From the storm to the sea

Not a silver crack this time,
white heat foaming with power
thundering down the glen from the hilltops
where the river was born.

Not a silver crack but the force
of life seeking the next vein or artery
urgent, possessive, bringing life and destruction
in equal measure.

The colour of water.
The forested banks.
Both caught in the flow
of this primal war dance.

White horses, black manes.
Riding the surging currents
diving with the dippers,
reaching for the pebbled bed.

Under the old bridge the new bridge
and out of the mouth into the wide,
                        wide
                                        sea.

documentarity

just press return
to enter
and watch the opening
of your blank stage
the last time
before the first blemish
your first change
starting with the traditional
then to the additional
then some shaping
then reshaping
cutting
culling
reinserting
then more shaping
now it's getting somewhere
now check it over
just to make sure
get a trusted opinion
look at it again
make all necessary changes
look at it again
make your final changes
save your final changes
and finally
just press return
to exit

New York Public Library

There is
a whole city
to play in
a whole day
to explore.
The warmth of
springtime
has turned, in a day,
the branches
from winter
to green.

The beat and the
brightness
the buildings
and basements
the beautiful,
bold, yet
terrible vision of what
money can make.

The museums list
themselves out;
their tours
and exhibits
and objects
lost and found.

I am drawn to the river
the bridges,
the banks of the East and the West.
I am drawn to the harbour and
garden squares and the first
chance to be, again,
outside, at a table
drinking.

But that is not what I choose.

The longings of wartime,
the peculiar patterns of
desire for books
lead me to the public library,
to the place of quiet,
a quiet
like that of the reverence of a
cathedral;
the quiet of heads bent over
words and pages,
like those in an attitude
of prayer.

As in the cathedrals
and chapels of great cities
so too the libraries hold
those who find this
is also a place to abide,
to sleep, to take

rest from
the hunger,
the cold.

Along the artists' walkway, forwards
up the marble steps,
past the white men and their pens
and the white women
who broke through onto
a white published page

to sit, white fingers flying
across a writing board
soul finding
its grounding again
in words.

Oblivious to where
I am in the world
other than that
there is reading,
and I am writing.

Again.

dance to survive

the desert seems unforgiving
and yet there is this
this stubborn thing
tsukunyuku tsukunyuku
ne mugwenga
the desert seems uninviting
and yet still there is this
this restless thing
bhubhurrr bhubhurrr
ne mudenga
and it almost always scorches
and it almost never dampens
and the dust just never settles
on the dancefloor of survival
tambai tambai tambai tambai
figures shape to perform
song to belong
dance for the dead
and when the twilight is right
you can see yourself in them
the most many and few
and when the twilight is right
you can see yourself the extent
the furthest far and near
almost always scorching
almost never dampening
dust just never settling

pangu pangu pangu pangu
kwangu kwangu kwangu kwangu
pangu pangu pangu pangu
kwangu kwangu kwangu kwangu

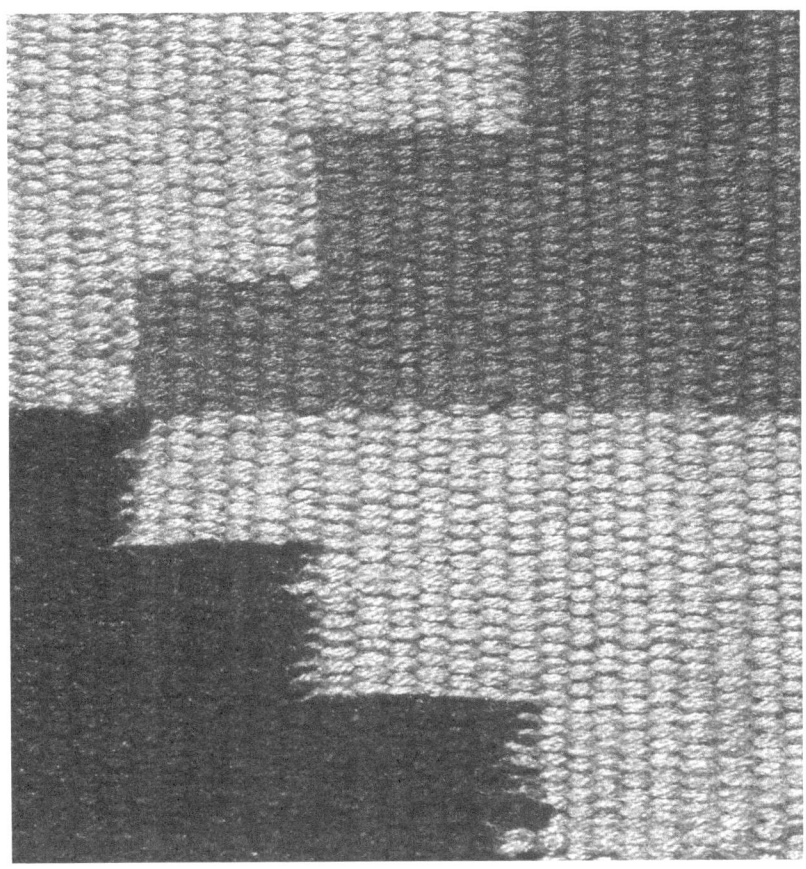

Desert museum

There is a sadness here,
translated by science
as a broken earth,
and disappeared people
are written back in to the desert.

Written back in,
in the past tense,
definite articles,
questions of wonderment
overlain with facts:
the weight of the saguaro;
the length of the bone;
the height of the temperature.
The warnings everywhere
pointing to our ways of measuring
the death of beauty.

It is wartime.
Brecht's painter is
a blonde-haired man
screaming death to what
his money has already
drained of life,
and of language.

I hear the young women next to me
speaking a laughing Arabic,

scarves fluttering in the breeze
gentled by the flowers
and sheltered by the silence
speaking of food as the baby sleeps.

A hummingbird sings with a sparrow.

All held by the deep silence
of the land,
brown,
    green
        and gold,
calling us to reverence,
calling through the ancestors,
calling to prayer.

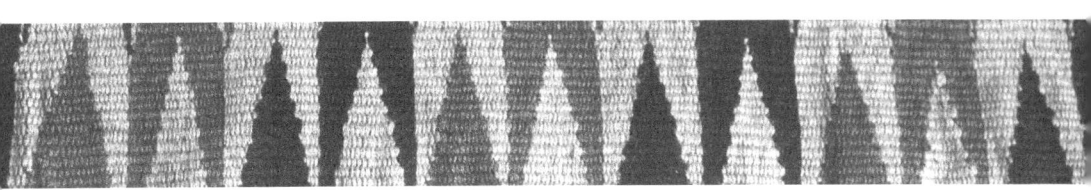

community

community is an organism
community is an organisation
community is unreal
community is an ideal
community is a sense
community has a fence
community will decide
community will deride
community is collective
community is selective
community is refined
community is defined
community is a word
community is a world

Visiting Mercy

For Hannah

Your gift was in the question
in a searching to repay
having questioned
and then pondered
you found the perfect way.

A meeting set for lunchtime
a little hesitant, unsure,
but ready for receiving
what the offering makes pure.

Like songlines in the city
you show me where the lines are drawn
between the richer
and the poorer and the
ones who live forlorn.

In these suburbs there are people
who are making all things well
those whose eyes dim into sadness
meeting all that love can tell.

In the garden and the classroom
in the office, on the walls,
tenacity and fruitfulness
are bringing down the walls.

They are showing us the reason
why our anger is so right
for the separations murder us
and keep hope out of sight.

But the lawyers and the families,
the lovers and the friends
are here, and clear, and witnessing
insisting on amends,

insisting on the justice
that restores the broken soul
offering back the dignity
that gives the lost a home.

We sit inside a restaurant
another sign of hope
of the journey into exile
and arriving with a jolt.

And in happy conversation
over bread and rice and tea
your gift is fully given
meeting gratitude in me.

wish i'd known better

last month i went to the gallery
to admire some art
but by the time i got there
someone had stolen the paintings

a few weeks ago i went to the library
to increase my knowledge
but by the time i got there
someone had borrowed the book

the other day i went to a concert
to have a good time
but by the time i got there
someone had spoilt the show

the other night i went to a fancy restaurant
to enjoy some fine cuisine
but by the time i got there
someone had burnt the food

just this morning i went to the doctor
to find out what's wrong with me
but by the time i got there
i was late for my appointment

one day i will go somewhere
to do something
but until i get there
someone has to grow

Healtime

For Raewyn

Dawn is violeting
the night sky.
Sleek in their blackCoats
and harsh of song
the rooks have left their
roost.

The stars flee,
setting as surely
as the sun rises.

From the pages
of my books the elders say
the way up is the way down.

Their voices
are lost to the years.
Their words
blackCoated
against a skyWhite page.

Keep falling
to rise.

Go down to
the river
to pray.

Take off your shoes.

To sow seeds,
you must be close to
rotting, blackened husks,

close to the dying
that will be living.

Kneel on the
turned earth
if you would plant
a garden.

But first,
for now,
lay down your head.

For it is still wartime.

Give yourself to the frailties
of dreamtime.

Healtime.
Then,
heal time.

And rise, sleekCoated
and harsh of song,
like the rooks
black-inking their
words against
the violet
of this day.

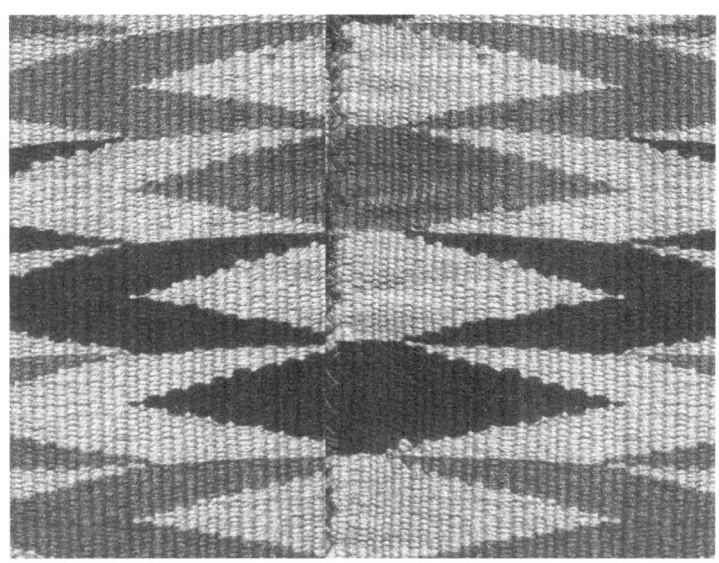

inWARdly

cannot say how it really started
but can see how it really ended up
something about the way it turned out
caused us to turn against ourselves
and we've been fighting ever since

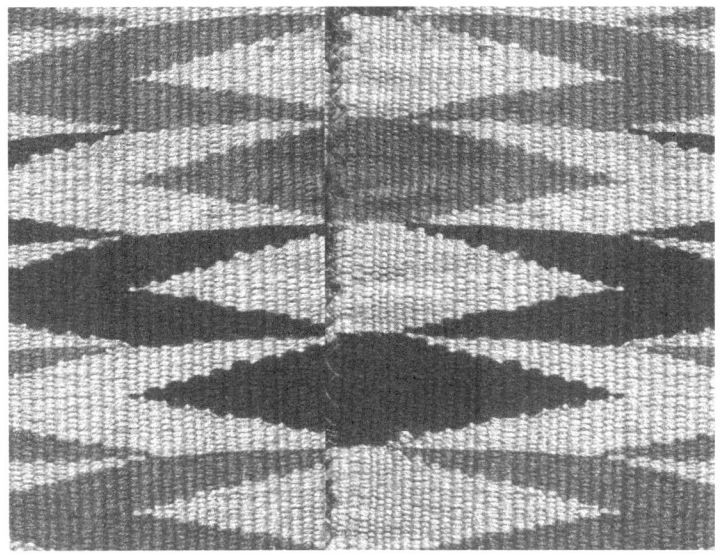

Courage is made in times like this

Courage is made in times
like this.
It is not
the pain I welcome,
but the certain knowledge
of healing;
it is not
the wounding I embrace,
but the ache of the scar
which stores the story;

it is not the loss
of blood
or skin
which makes me linger
on the knife edge
of fear, close to
the disaster that
is anger;
it is the
lack of courtesy
with which some arrows
are unleashed,
the ones
which simply refuse
to follow
the rules
of love
or war.

look right look left

look right
look left
look right once more
before you cross the border
wait on the side
the man onscreen has to decide
which suit to wear
green means go
proceed right in
next
amber means wait
we are dealing with your case
next
red means stop
there is no safe passage
look right
look left
look right once more
before you cross the border

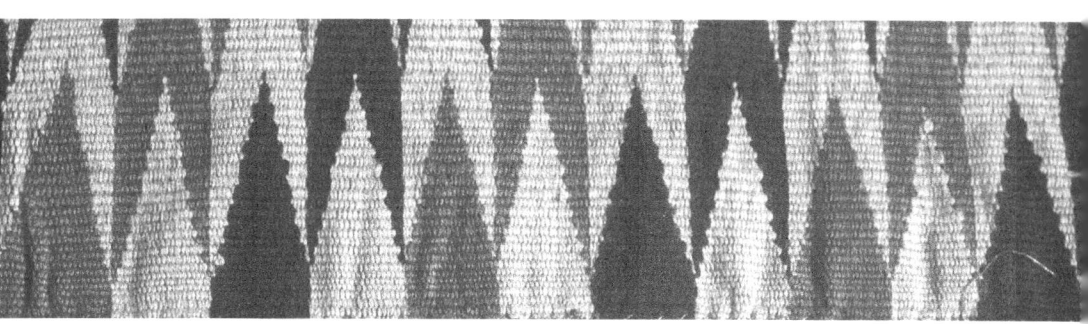

We will not let you pass

For Agbashie

We will not let you pass.
We will require of you
a birth certificate,
a passport,
a non-refundable ticket,
insurance,
inoculation.
We will require of you £3,500
for the promise
of processing your visa on time.

But We will not process your visa on time.

We will not do this.
This, We will not do.

For the same application;
the identical sponsorship letter
for this
We will make a decision
which is arbitrary.

10 We will allow to pass.
7 We will not decide.
We will not decide.
We will not return your papers.

you have no power.
you have no voice.

This We will do.

We will deny your audience
the delight of your dancing.

We will not let you pass.

We will separate you from
your sisters and brothers,
from your mothers and fathers

and to those who dared to ask
who dared to believe,
they too We will frustrate.

We will not let you pass.

We will

We will not.

We will not
let
    you
        pass.

meet me at the corner

meet me at the corner
and we can act as if we're free
pretend that it doesn't hurt
the way it used to hurt

meet me at the corner
in defiance of ourselves
but don't speak of truth
only brings despair

meet me at the corner
bring all your relatives
scabs and memories
tears and strategies

come let's meet
where lines meet
bring all your corners
so they can meet

An upper room

In my tradition
there is
an upper room.

Just another
ordinary story
of a faithful, dusty walk
taken by friends
along many a road
together,
then apart.

Just an ordinary story
of an edgy meal
on the edges of time.

Its threads tell of
a breaking
a betraying
a cleansing
a pausing
of praising
and passion
of healing
conversing,
accusing,
then
leaving.

Windows open
to the sharpening air.

Dreams caught
in the
entanglements.

Nerves fray
and fail.

Meekness inherits
on this blade edge
of knowing
and as the sword pierces
it is accomplished.

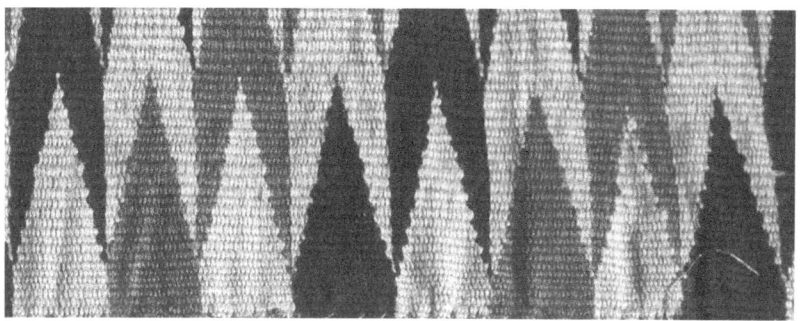

my-views-news reporter

floating in from the neon sky
comes that gentle alien
armed with x-ray and flashing smile
and goodies for the kids

sneaking in through the front door
the undercover reporter
smuggled across the border
rickety ride with chickens and goats
and a hi-tech recorder

sitting in
in squalor among real people
the investigative journalist
soliciting selected truths
done well to learn the local lingo
but it's still hard to tell
whether they're a reuter or a writer

going in to the gist of it
a brave correspondent
the exposer of truth
representative of curiosity
affirmer of suspicions
precursor of eventualities

here is the propaganda
read by
whoever is on duty
over to the one out in the field
then back to you in the studio
the programme for your memory
here's basis for your argument
in future conversations

After this restless house

(The Oresteia)

All afternoon and all evening
the family tore itself
    apart.
Blood flowed behind the scenes
and spilled

over in rivers
    of screaming
vengeance
and through the
insatiable wounds
of grief,
and ambition. Men

declared war, to possess
women, and women

drove knives into their men.

Everywhere
was grief,
and trouble,

and the people,

and the land,
had no rest

under the nightmarish skies
of wilfully fateful vengeance.

Every now and then the child
would appear,
in her yellow dress
and with a suitcase –
of herbs,
we were told –
a ghost now,
but also a witness.

In times of war
sometimes rest
can only come when
the grief screams into death
with such deafening silence,
that a child's voice
of remembrance
can actually be heard.

'Rosemary for it.
And a shell for my father,
and a posy for my mother,
and gifts for my brother
and my witnessing sister
and for you.'

And then the cloth,
and the teacups,
and an offer of hospitality,

an honest memory
of what was
and what was not,

and the tragic recognition,
coming as the heart steadies,
that what we have done
and who we are
have become one.

She pours out the tea into
tiny play cups.

'It can be whatever you want it to be.'

Wine,
palm wine,
juice,
water.

It is what brings the family back
to table, back
to conversation, back
into a world where words
can have enough meaning
to live by
and to heal.

I leave the theatre
empty of it all save for the
simple understanding

that I can live
with the contradictions,
with the guilt,
with the blood of this war
on my hands too and
with the witnessing,

if
  every now
  and then

I can sit on the ground
with a love cup
and forgiving company,

and drink.

new dogs old tricks

see them prance
with tails up
ready to impress themselves
with the same old routine
best thing for themselves
rather than the right thing
only let go
of what they choose
not what they should
it's the same old situation
old tricks
but not as old as this
young guns
but not as young as this
wonder how they feel
wonder what they think
can't say they are embarrassed
or else shame
would have driven them
can't say they care
or else compassion
would have moved them
can't say they are decent
or else morality
would have forced them
so it's more puppies
fresh from the pound

thoroughbred to stay ahead
ready again
to perform the same
so see the latest presentation
now showing
featuring the biting dogs
that seldom bark

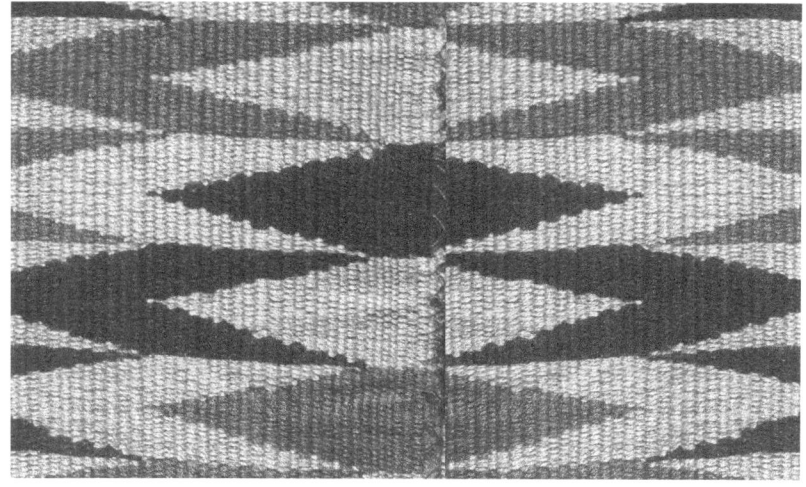

The one you feed

All the thoughts paraded
through her mind.
The ones wishing harm.
The ones wishing revenge.
The ones calculating tests,
to elicit proofs,
to be sure,
just to be certain sure.

The ones wanting more
than enough.

Deliberate,
    dainty
        diminishments
pinpointing a time,
extracting words, choosing
the precise place for
the inflicting of pain.

From the hurt within,
came the planning
of a feast for the wolf,
the hungry one lurking
always by the path,
tongue lolling, teeth wide and
knowingly expectant.

'Feed me,' said the wolf.
'I need more of your bile. Make me
grow fat on your misery, your
pain, your desire to get even.'

All the thoughts paraded
through the battlefield of her mind.

not meant for words

things not meant for words
are what they are
sights meant for eyes
sounds meant for ears
knowledge for the conscience
stories of the heart

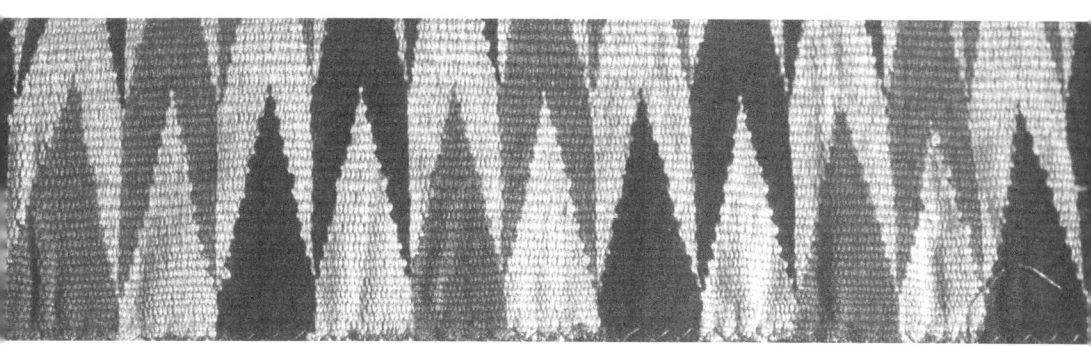

The end of reason

The necessity for protection and
priority gives reason all power.

To know the power of reason is
to know and find
respect for the wild things.

It is diminishment and discipline.

It is necessary cost.

We understand
standing under
its authoritative voice.

Nature retreats
to a safe

    distance.

But in the language of poetry
there is also this to tell:
the power and victory of reason
is not where our arrows were made,
is not the fire where they wait
for the warrior's skin.

Reason is not the only
war story.

taBlets

in the friction of conviction
tongues jostling for position
under the command of minds
with more views than windows

I went to the trees

I went to the trees
to breathe
but the bark
was smooth silver
and the bark
was rough dark.

So I found my breath
taken by the leaves
by the way they lit the hills,
glittering in the sunlight
like arrowheads.

I went to the trees,
to the leaves
to the branches and bark
to breathe.

But the skin.

The skin.

The scarred and wounding
skin.

voice versa

they used to sing
or used to sin
depends who you listen to

they saved savages
or vandalised villages
depends who you hear from

this is a community
or a commodity
depends what you buy into

this is a birthmark
or a trademark
depends what you invest in

this is something
or some other something
depends
just depends

This music

The first sound sends an arrow
straight to the womb,
sends seeds scattering
across the soil,
spinning the soul out into the
skies, into the night's starlight
along Orion's belt,
across the Pleiades
and over the bright
pathways of the Milky Way.

From Venus to the Pole Star
holding the Plough
then plunging again,
deep into the earth,
turning through soil,
piercing the crust, the mantle
and penetrating
the core.
Molten now, making all that
is to be made,
hiding all that must stay hidden.

The touch emboldens, the sound
slips itself onto the fingertips
as melody, clumsy, yet careful
and contained as I am thoroughly
found, played, and made again
in music.

The hunters are here,
the warriors who do not fight,
the arrows in the fire
the scars made on the skin
the *moko* and the markings
the words of all languages
the kisses of all lovers
the skins of creatures, white and black,
the songs of all separations,
all celebrations.

Every fire tended and
each loaf taken, torn and shared.
Wine is here and cool water.
And somewhere, deep inside,
if you listen in closely,
comes the start of the dance.

The bone bends to the music
blood beats a path into the worlds
of the dead,
of the unborn
of the dying
and the loving
and the wisdom in living.

The body bows towards the music
towards the wood, towards the table,
eyes lowered and
with reverence towards the ground,

sensing the fallen leaves of autumn,
the lacing frosts of winter,
the shoots of spring,
the dripping abundance
of summer,
her fruits,
her harvest.

This sound,
this sound is spring water,
is quenching of soul-thirst.

This music is meat and meal
and maize and madness.

This tune brings trance and trembling
treasures and terror.

From this root
comes all the music
of the world.

border

between
connecting
separating
line
drawn
in sand
in chalk
in pen
in accent
in thought
a button
pressed
a stamp
depressed
inclined
or
to decline
hardening
need to be
softening
need to be
dissolving

Daffodils

For the first time
the daffodils do not
bring me cheerfulness,
their nodding yellow heads
incongruent, stubborn,
sunshine at the wrong
end of winter.

It is wartime.
The earth wrestles against the seedcorn.
The ploughed fields
may or may not see harvest.

There are old gun emplacements
on the clifftops, looking
across the estuary to
the nuclear power plant.

Around their concrete bases
the same jaundiced flowers.
Springs heralds or signs of
our fear?

I do not know whether to fight
or to flee. I do not know if the
East wind will spread pollen
or freeze away the first hope of life.

On the borders of Europe they are
herding people into cages and sending them
back to the bombs.

On the borders of this field
there are daffodils, nodding away
as the bodies wash again, out to sea.

broken world, broken word

the land
this land
is our land

the land
this land
is our land

the land
this land
is our land

the land
this land
is our land

the land
this land
all this land
our land
on the land
this land
our land
we walk
we grow
we build
we survive

the land
this land
all this land
our land
on the land
this land
our land
we care
we cry
we forgive
we sweep

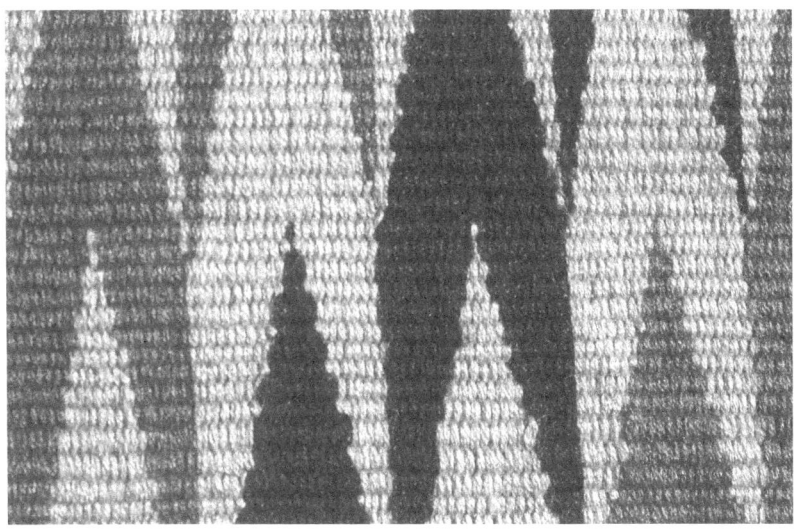

The spring

Across the air of the uplands,
under the mist,
under the winter sun,
following the sweep of the rain,
soaring with hope, with
exuberance, under clouds of
white and bronze,
he comes to her,
feather-like,
with a question.

Kneeling
at the source,
skin on cold stone
hands cupped
holding just enough
sweetness for the lips
to taste the first fruits
and to tell out the greatness
and strength of the
making, moving earth.

Her answer is the sound
of clear water
ringing joyously
from the
side of the hill,

humble for this season,
spilling her song over the
water table
announcing her love of
life with such confidence
that it is as if, once more,
a saviour has been born.

Acknowledgements

We wish to acknowledge the many colleagues, friends, family members, mystics and fellow travellers who have been companions, guides and wayfarers. Without the generous hospitality of many people – the provisioning with food, shelter and wisdom – the border-crossings could not have been made.

Without the administrative care of Lauren Roberts and Bella Hoogeveen the journeys could not have been taken.

The following friends and colleagues, in no special order, brought words and forms for which we are full of gratitude: Gameli Tordzro, Naa Densua Tordzro, Julien Danero, Robert Gibb, Prue Holmes, Mariam Attia, Jane Andrews, Richard Fay, Sarah Craig, Karin Zwaan, Chantelle Warner, David Gramling, Ross White, Obed Kasule, Rosco Kasujja, Maria Grazia Imperiale, Giovanna Fassetta, Judith Reynolds, Melissa Chaplin, Lyn Ma, Katja Frimberger, Charles Forsdick, Kofi Agyekum, Kofi Anyidoho, Nazmi Al-Masri, Aileen Ritchie and the Ignite Theatre Company, Nii-Tete Yartey and the Noyam Institute for African Dance, Glasgow Refugee, Asylum and Migration Network, Seeds of Thought, the Iona Community.

The opportunity to perform, air and interrupt lectures with the poetry in this collection was generously provided by University of Glasgow, Keele University, Stirling University, Centre for Contemporary Arts Glasgow, Glasgow Centre for Population Health, Glasgow School of Art, Heriot-Watt University, University of Arizona, Islamic University of Gaza, University College London, Cologne University, Te Whaiti School, Te Urewera, University of Waikato, Auckland University of Technology, University of Auckland, University of South Australia, University of Melbourne, Victoria University Wellington, University of Victoria (British Columbia), Buenos Aires Museum of Immigration, Hong

Kong Polytechnic University, British University Dubai, Maryhill Integration Network, Woodlands Community Gardens, House for an Art Lover, Calais refugee camps.

The work was funded with the support of the Arts & Humanities Research Council Translating Cultures Large Grant: Researching Multilingually at the Borders of Language, the Body, Law and the State. AHRC Grant Ref: AH/L006936/1.

To all at Wild Goose Publications, our humble thanks for working with these words and publishing them on your beautiful pages.

For those who remained at home with their love as we travelled, wrote, made and spirited forth the work – Tarneem, Robert, Rima – words for sufficient gratitude fail us – as they should.

Alison Phipps and Tawona Sitholé

Wild Goose Publications is part of the Iona Community:

- An ecumenical movement of men and women from different walks of life and different traditions in the Christian church
- Committed to the gospel of Jesus Christ, and to following where that leads, even into the unknown
- Engaged together, and with people of goodwill across the world, in acting, reflecting and praying for justice, peace and the integrity of creation
- Convinced that the inclusive community we seek must be embodied in the community we practise

Together with our staff, we are responsible for:

- Our islands residential centres of Iona Abbey, the MacLeod Centre on Iona, and Camas Adventure Centre on the Ross of Mull

and in Glasgow:
- The administration of the Community
- Our work with young people
- Our publishing house, Wild Goose Publications
- Our association in the revitalising of worship with the Wild Goose Resource Group

www.ionabooks.com

The Iona Community was founded in Glasgow in 1938 by George MacLeod, minister, visionary and prophetic witness for peace, in the context of the poverty and despair of the Depression. Its original task of rebuilding the monastic ruins of Iona Abbey became a sign of hopeful rebuilding of community in Scotland and beyond. Today, we are about 250 Members, mostly in Britain, and 1500 Associate Members, with 1400 Friends worldwide. Together and apart, 'we follow the light we have, and pray for more light'.

For information on the Iona Community contact:
The Iona Community, 21 Carlton Court,
Glasgow G5 9JP, UK. Phone: 0141 429 7281
e-mail: admin@iona.org.uk; web: www.iona.org.uk

For enquiries about visiting Iona, please contact:
Iona Abbey, Isle of Iona, Argyll PA76 6SN, UK. Phone: 01681 700404
e-mail: ionacomm@iona.org.uk

Wild Goose Publications, the publishing house of the Iona Community established in the Celtic Christian tradition of Saint Columba, produces books, e-books, CDs and digital downloads on:

- holistic spirituality
- social justice
- political and peace issues
- healing
- innovative approaches to worship
- song in worship, including the work of the Wild Goose Resource Group
- material for meditation and reflection

For more information:

Wild Goose Publications
21 Carlton Court,
Glasgow G5 9JP, UK

Tel. +44 (0)141 429 7281
e-mail: admin@ionabooks.com

or visit our website at
www.ionabooks.com
for details of all our products and online sales